Kids Book of Questions:

How Do Things Fly?

SPEEDY PUBLISHING LLC

Speedy Publishing LLC
40 E. Main St. #1156
Newark, DE 19711
www.speedypublishing.com

ISBN: 978-1-6814-5437-5

First Printed 03/25/2015

Animals That Fly

Some animals can fly because they have WINGS. A wing is a type of fin with a surface that produces force for flight through the atmospher or air. Wings are common in all type of birds. Some insects do have wings as well. Wings are used by animals to migrate.

Next pages are examples of animals with wings so they can fly.

Parrot

Tucan

Kingfisher

Owl

Pied Bush Chat

Asian Fairy Bluebird

Gull

Mosquito

Flies

Hissing Cockroaches

Terns

Bat

Dragonfly

Butterfly

Flamingo

Cockroach

Ladybug

Bees

List other animals you know that have wings.

Other Things That Fly

Some things fly as well because of their wings, like the airplane and the kite.

Some things may not have wings but still fly, like the hot air balloon and the balloons. In a hot air balloon, a gas burner is used to heat air to a temperature of about 212°F. Since hot air is lighter and less dense than the cool air around the balloon, the heated air causes the whole balloon to rise.

Hot Air Balloon

Kite

Airplane

Balloons

www.ingramcontent.com/pod-product-compliance
Lightning Source LLC
LaVergne TN
LVHW060830170826
845678LV00010B/1940
* 9 7 9 8 8 6 9 4 5 5 5 9 8 *